D1118172

How Marten Got His Spots
& Other Kootenai Indian Stories

How Marten Got His Spots

& Other Kootenai Indian Stories

Developed by the
Kootenai Culture Committee
Confederated Salish and Kootenai Tribes

Illustrated by
Debbie Joseph Finley
Howard Kallowatt, Jr.

Co-published by
Salish Kootenai College Press, Pablo, Montana
&
Montana Historical Society Press, Helena, Montana

Originally published as *How Marten Got His Spots, Coyote and Trout, Little Weasel's Dream,* and *Tepee Making* in **The Indian Reading Series** by the Pacific Northwest Indian Program, Joseph Coburn, Director, Northwest Regional Educational Laboratory, Portland, Oregon.

Cover drawing by Debbie Joseph Finley.
Cover design by Wyatt Design, Helena, MT.

Library of Congress Cataloging-in-Publication Data:
How Marten got his spots : & other Kootenai Indian stories / developed by the Kootenai Culture Committee, Confederated Salish and Kootenai Tribes ; illustrated by Debbie Joseph Finley, Howard Kallowatt, Jr.
    v. cm.
    Stories originally published separately as How Martin got his spots, Coyote and Trout, Little Weasel's dream, and Tepee making in The Indian reading series by the Pacific Northwest Indian Program, Northwest Regional Educational Laboratory, Portland, Or., c1978-c1981.
    Contents: How Marten got his spots -- Coyote and Trout -- Little Weasel's dream -- Tepee making.
ISBN 0-917298-92-6
    1. Kutenai Indians--Folklore. 2. Tales--Montana. [1. Kutenai Indians--Folklore. 2. Indians of North America--Montana--Folklore. 3. Folklore--Montana.] I. Finley, Debbie Joseph, 1953- ill. II. Kallowatt, Howard, ill. III. Confederated Salish and Kootenai Tribes of the Flathead Reservation, Kootenai Culture Committee.
E99.K85 H68 2002
398.2'089'973--dc21

                                                        2002075925

This printing reset and reprinted 2002 by
Salish Kootenai College Press
Box 117
Pablo, MT 59855
&
Montana Historical Society Press
Box 201201
Helena, MT 59620

Printed in Canada

Table of Contents

How Marten Got His Spots

M arten and Mink were brothers.

Since Mink was the oldest, he took care of his younger brother, Marten.

Mink gave strict orders to Marten.

"Whatever you do, never go over the hill," he said.

"Always stay close to home."

Marten would look up at the hill and wonder why he wasn't allowed to play on the other side.

One day his curiosity got the best of him.

He went to the top of the hill.

Down in the valley was a tepee.

Marten wondered who lived there.

As he got closer, he saw Bear working in the yard.

When Bear went back into the tepee,
Marten followed her in and sat down across
from her.

Bear offered Marten a wooden dish full of
pemmican.

As Marten reached across the fire to take
the dish, Bear grabbed his arm and pulled
him into the fire!

Just in time, he scrambled out of the fire
before he scorched himself too badly.

Poor Marten ran all the way home and
jumped under the covers.

When Mink returned from hunting, there
was no sign of Marten.

Mink looked everywhere.

Finally, he lifted up the blankets and found
his little brother.

Marten told Mink he had not listened and had gone over the hill.

He explained what had happened and showed his big brother the burnt spots on his fur.

For a few days, Mink put medicine on his brother's wounds until only scars remained.

And that's how martens got their spots.

Coyote and Trout

One winter day, Coyote went for a walk by a lake.

He saw a woman standing not too far away.

He thought to himself, "I will walk by and have a closer look."

As he got near, the woman said, "Coyote, come over here and wrestle with me!"

"Ha!" said Coyote. "You must be kidding! I am too strong!"

The woman got hold of Coyote and they wrestled.

Finally, Coyote went down.

He was dead!

Meanwhile, Fox, who had been traveling here and there, realized he hadn't seen Coyote for quite awhile.

He knew something must be wrong.

So, being a faithful friend, he went looking for Coyote.

Fox came to the shore of the lake.

There he found Coyote's body.

Fox used his powers to bring Coyote back to life.

With no shame at all, Coyote told how the woman had knocked him out.

Coyote and Fox left together but hadn't gone too far when they became separated.

Coyote wandered back to the place by the lake.

Again the lady asked Coyote to wrestle with her.

But this time it would be different, because Coyote's powers told him not to get knocked out.

It hurt Coyote when she threw him down.

He almost passed out.

He was so still, the woman thought she had killed him.

She turned to run.

Coyote jumped up and tried to grab her, but he missed.

The woman ran down to the lake as Coyote chased her.

The lake was covered with ice except for a small hole.

The woman jumped through the hole, with Coyote right behind!

When she was under the water, she turned into a trout.

She turned Coyote into a trout, too, and married him.

Every morning the trout would leave camp.

When they returned, they would have some meat.

This made Coyote very curious because
he was greedy and wanted some meat.

One morning Coyote told his wife, "Let
me help you bring in the food."

It was all right with her, so he went along.

They came to a place where some pieces
of meat were dangling in the water.

Coyote looked for the biggest piece.

When he found it, he grabbed the string
with his mouth, pulled, and broke it off.

He did this all morning.

From then on, Coyote went with the trout every day.

Soon he had all the meat, and the other trout had none.

Meanwhile, Fox, who had been traveling everywhere, heard that the trout were starving.

Right away, Fox knew that Coyote was behind it all.

Fox made a fish line out of tough sinew.

The next day, he went fishing.

The trout were already biting.

Fox threw in his line, hoping to catch Coyote.

Coyote grabbed the line because it had the biggest piece of meat.

He tried to break the line, but he couldn't.

Fox pulled his friend out of the water.

He took a big club and pretended he was going to kill Coyote.

Coyote yelled, "Don't kill me! I'm your friend, Coyote."

Fox mocked him saying, "Don't kill me! I'm your friend, Coyote."

He then asked Coyote, "Why did you do this?"

Coyote said, "I married a trout and have been living in the water with them. I didn't mean to harm anyone."

Fox said to Coyote, "You were almost killed because you tried to take all the meat and left nothing for others.

"This should teach you not to be so greedy."

Little Weasel's Dream

▲▲▲▲▲▲▲▲▲

*I*t was the middle of August. The berries were ripe and ready for picking. A party of seven women decided to take their children whortleberry picking. They planned to go up into the mountains behind Lone Pine.

They had to travel by horseback. They
loaded their picking baskets on the horses.
The children had to ride double and even
triple. The younger children rode with their
mothers.

The women and children rode for many
hours until they found a spot with enough
berries to fill their baskets. They stopped,
unloaded their baskets, and piled them near
the berry patch.

They tied their horses to nearby trees
and gave them enough lead rope to graze.

Someone saw signs of wild animals, so
they had to be extra careful. The children

were given strict orders to stay close together near the elders. The older children were expected to watch the younger ones.

The women were so busy picking that they forgot about everything else. Late in the afternoon when the baskets were full, they decided it was time to start home. The women told the children to get ready for the long, slow trip home.

One of the women noticed that she hadn't seen her three-year-old son, Little Weasel, for quite some time. She became alarmed when she found that no one else had seen him either. The women and children began looking all over for Little Weasel.

    Little Weasel was playing and having such a fun time that he didn't realize he had wandered too far and was lost. When he realized he was lost, he began running, desperately trying to find his mother. He couldn't find his mother or anyone else. He sat down on a log and began to cry.

Suddenly, he heard branches breaking
behind him. When he turned around, he
saw a big, black bear coming towards him.
Little Weasel was very frightened.

He began to scream for help as loudly as he could. The women were about to give up their search and send for help from their village. Then they heard Little Weasel cry out for his mother. She ran to him, picked him up, and held him in her arms. She was so happy that her son was safe.

Little Weasel told his mother that he was playing and became lost. When he realized that he was lost, he began to cry. Exhausted, he fell asleep by a log. Little Weasel thought that a big black bear was about to get him when he cried out.

As it turned out, Little Weasel was just dreaming and learned a great lesson from his dream. This should be a lesson to all children: Mind your elders.

Tepee Making

*L*ong ago, tepees were made out of buffalo or deer hides. Today many tepees are made out of canvas.

When Indian women make a tepee, they do a lot of cutting and sewing. The women will cut the material and sew it together piece by piece.

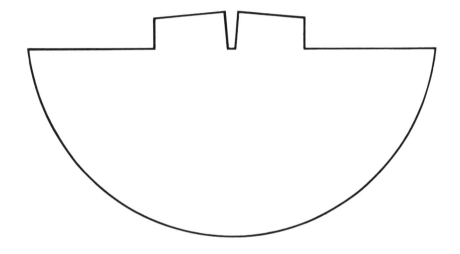

When the sewing is done, the women will check the shape and size of the tepee. The back of the tepee should be a little shorter than the front. A round hole is cut in the front to be used as a door. The tepee will have two flaps in the front at the top of the tepee. These flaps will be used to keep wind and rain out. They can be closed when the weather is bad. When a fire is built inside the tepee, the flaps can be opened to let the smoke out.

Lodgepole pine trees are used for tepee poles. The branches are cut off and the bark is peeled from the trees. The poles should be long and straight. Some large tepees use as many as fifteen poles.

Four poles are tied together near the top. They are set up to form a pyramid, then three poles are added to each side with two in the front of the doorway. When all poles

are put in place, the frame will begin to form the shape of a tepee. Two poles are always used to open and close the flaps at the top of the tepee.

The canvas is tied to a single pole. This pole is then placed at the rear of the frame. The canvas is unfolded and wrapped around the frame. When all the poles are covered, the canvas will fit loosely over them.

Above the door opening, there are two rows of holes. Wooden pegs are put through these holes to close the tepee.

The poles are pushed outward to make the tepee snug. After this is done, wooden stakes are pounded through canvas loops at the bottom of the tepee. These stakes hold the tepee to the ground so it won't tip over. Finally, the door opening is covered with a flap.

Tepee making takes a lot of hard work and skill. A tight-fitting tepee will not leak and looks nice. Indian women are proud when they make a nice looking tepee.

Kootenai tepees today are not painted as they were years ago. The Kootenai Indians painted animals and birds on their tepees. The kind of animal painted on a tepee meant the owner's spirit was like that particular animal. It may have been a bear, deer, buffalo, or some other animal or bird.

Some tepees were painted with a ripple design, a symbol of green grass.

Other designs were mainly for decorative purposes, more or less to beautify the tepee.

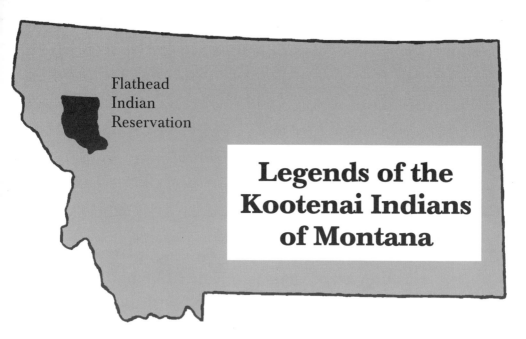

Legends of the Kootenai Indians of Montana

Flathead Indian Reservation

The home of the Kootenai or Ksanka Nation is in the northern Rocky Mountains, centered in what is now northern Montana, northern Idaho, and southeastern British Columbia. Our band is the southernmost of the seven Kootenai bands and resides on the Flathead Indian Reservation in northwest Montana.

Before Europeans came to the area, fish were abundant in the rivers and lakes; deer, buffalo, and other game were in the mountains and plains; and berries and roots filled these valleys. It is a vast area, but our people traveled easily with canoes, horses, and dogs. For centuries the Kootenai lived with the abundance of this land and cared for it.

Stories and games taught the young the values and wisdom of the elders. Some of these stories explained how greed, arrogance, and failure to respect the tribal community would lead to disgrace. Other legends taught about the habits and characteristics of the game animals that supported the tribe. The stories were entertainment, but they were also education. Storytelling was especially important during the winter when nights were long and cold in the northern Rocky Mountains.

Through this book, these stories are now available to children everywhere, to share in the traditional values of Kootenai Indian storytellers.